re-Mothering
Poems by Susan Chast

re-Mothering

Poems by Susan Chast

Spider House Publishing
2015

The cover image is a photo of a bronze plaque that artist Agostino Agostinelli made from a crayon drawing by Susan Chast. The poem "Mums" first appeared in *The First Day*, Vol 1:3 (Spring 2014).

First Printing: 2015

ISBN 978-1-329-12148-5

Spider House Publishing
PO Box 485
Lansdowne, PA 19050

info@spiderhousepublishing.com

Dedication

To my mother, artist Dot Chast, with love.

Green

Mom walks and talks paint
in the yellow blue white forest
and brings the trees home.

Acknowledgements

Thank you to my mother Dot Chast for letting me intersperse her tiny sketches among my poems; to Nancy Kathan for her gift of design; to Cindy Palmer for being my first reader, editor and proofreader; and to Christina Whitt for the photography.

I also owe gratitude to poet Alison Hicks and my peers in her Philadelphia Wordshop and to the many online groups that nourished my writing since I retired from teaching in 2012, especially *Poets United*, *The Imaginary Garden with Real Toads* and *The dVerse Poets Pub*. Scores of poets inspired me and commented on my work. And I could not have completed this book without the support of the Buddies of Jesus and family and friends. You know who you are. Thank you.

I owe very special thanks to Jennifer Elam for encouragement during our weekly writing sessions and for collaborating on our book *Taking a Walk with God*.

Susan L. Chast

10 May 2015

Contents

Preface

To "re-mother" is to nurture, a mothering not outgrown by crossing the line from childhood into adulthood. Like falling in love with the same person again and again, re-mothering once is not enough. Renewal is necessary.

We receive re-mothering from friends, family, companions in faith, loves, therapists, elements of nature and books we read. We re-mother others, too—not perfectly, but certainly instinctually. Instinct to mother is neither gender nor species bound. It grows from acceptance of the self. Ironically, I often neglect to re-mother myself. At home, I am reminded by my cat Miracle—who also tells me to feed her and to water the plants. I am reminded by God's still small voice and by Jesus who tries to bring out the mother in me and keep me honest and active.

The earth also re-mothers. The summer I spent on a mum farm—no pun intended—taught me that, as my poem "Mums" attests:

Mums

Back when I was sane
I labored at the Mum Farm.

No.

Back when I was insane
I labored at the Mum Farm
to find what I had lost.

No.
It's hard to tell the truth.

Back then I found myself
squatting between rows of color
knees and hands brown from being
kind to roots and buds while

upper teeth held my bottom lip
and a drop of saliva waited
to parallel salty ones
from the corners of my eyes.

Back then, sweat from my forehead
moistened my forearms, my shirt stuck
to my back, and my hands found
the healing heart of the Mother.

Mother Earth shows me a face of God. She is a book
without words that I read, walk on and ground myself in. I try to
take care of her as well as she does me.

Part One ~ Growing

Mom

Not Valentine's Day cards
and ultimately not songs, though
both speak when I cannot
get close enough, as you did always
in the kitchen, school room,
playground and art gallery
where your drawings on my inner
and outer walls took me
through life's growth
until big enough to see you
tall as the trees you love, rooted
and reaching beyond the sky.

It is enough, I think, to know
mutual admiration art to art,
poor copies of the human heart.

Precious

The three-year old greets people
as if fireflies in darkness,
soap bubbles aloft or
dandelion gold in green settings.

She is herself a blossom
bursting with silk-petal-covered
secrets and scents
of earth and sweetness.

She runs laughing as
people reach to pick her up,
as if a rose budding
in a patch of thorns.

Mother watches
her daughter as if
fine crystal balanced
on earth's edges.

The Climbing Tree

Mom drew the long-limbed pine while I watched chipmunks
and fairies run and hide from me in reindeer-mossed
hobbit homes under the brown-skinned roots
of the ancient tree, surrounded with rattlesnake-filled
stone walls where cows once grazed in the old days.
I climbed quietly to a still low limb to scout until pine
tickled my nose into a sneeze.

Later I dreamed untamed forests full of elves, lost
ghosts knocking on our walls and windows, and magic
so loud I couldn't sleep and, indeed, the morning footprints
dotted across the driveway could have been elf horses
and not two deer trespassing to chew lettuce
with the rabbits, little Peter Cottontail in the lead
as they ran before the morning sun.

I leaned my rake against the fence, clothes pinned
the towels on the line until they swept the ground
and scolded the crows and red-winged blackbirds,
robins, and starlings and swifts not to eat
mulberries over the fresh wet wash and to leave
some on the tree for me to eat with milk before
I visited the climbing tree.

Was it gone? Did it Brigadoon away when the night
moon played tricks on pathways and tree limbs?
One more rise, to climb and then another—
I knew it was closer yesterday, but not as close as when
my older brother or mom came along to play or when
the fairies slipped a dime under my pillow
in exchange for a tooth.

Now, where did fairies put the teeth? I scuffed
the thick mat of rusty needles to find them, reached
into nooks and climbed higher to see if
they hid my teeth up in the tree. And I heard mom
laugh at me, but she also told me stories of
when grandfather's geese cornered her, bit her
heels and chased her home.

That is when Rip Van Winkle started bowling,
the skies turned angry with fat cheeks blowing
hard to shake us from the limbs—and this time
everyone ran: elves and fairies, mom and brother
and me, deer, rabbit, horses, ghosts, leaves and rattle
snakes just like the cards in Alice's trial falling
and leaping for shelter and towels and naps and dreams.

Campfire

The moths are not fooled
by reflected light, they go
for heat all the time

Two now play around
her marshmallow on its twig
dangerously close to the fire.

The trees hold their breath
and beg the winds to lay low
while flesh and wings may singe.

Suddenly, smoke swirls
ash in her eyes. *"Mom!"* she calls,
blind and coughing, *"Help!"*

"Rabbit rabbit." Mom
whispers and hoses the fire
out. *"Good night!"* she blows

kisses to the trees,
moon and her child, saying
"We'll save sun for morning, my Dear."

Going to bed is easier
now than then when she, too,
was a moth near flame.

Companions

She started hugging trees when a toddler
    running to the lowest branch.

Tree skin in bark texture felt like her own
    protective layer: leather shoes and corduroys,
    tangled curls and earth-lined nails.

She wondered if punctured trees bled and
    peeling bark hurt, but only experimented on
    unattached twigs at marshmallow roasts.

Trees planted at her birth grew with her,
    helped her to read, cry, hide and sing
    in arms that held birds and crawling things,
    in limbs that stretched to touch clouds and stars.

She learned her strength from the heart of her tree
    how to long and how to persist silently.

Storms

Read her forehead to be forewarned.
Easy!
She can only keep secrets from herself.
Don't ruin her surprise—when she knows what
she feels, she'll let you know, and how!
Queasy?
Breathe through the fear until you reach delight.

She's a provocateur; she can't help it.
She stirs the pot and tastes every bit
of the soup herself searching for insight.
And then, wild horses couldn't keep her
from spilling the beans. No censure can stop
her *but-But-BUT* questions through quivering lips,
childlike eagerness and naked pleasure.

Drive Ways

Before bicycles
took over, entire
villages lived
in broken gravel:
The sides of hands
meticulously
carved out roads
and intersections
for the routes of
die-cast cars, vans
and scratched-paint
pick-up trucks.

Plastic tracks on rugs
couldn't compete
with dirt tracks,
scratched knees
and smudged shirts
making and
remaking towns
after anger stomped
or real cars rolled
them away
like sand paintings
in the winds of time.

Play Flowers

Grandmother's flower garden was as wild
as crazy quilts, a delight to a child
who made up stories, and myths compiled
of adventures fairies might love to ride.

Take snapdragons who lived with soft lamb's ear,
who outlasted weeds and repelled the deer—
They had a bright pink roar and mouths to fear
so taming one meant no danger came near.

Lamb's ear, as soft as silk, made evening wraps
that kept out chills and prevented collapse
if elves took dragons walking without caps
or fox fur gloves to keep their hands intact.

Dragons felt that weeds were nothing but blight,
so snarled and snapped at them to force their flight
but lamb's ear liked the tall green stems all right
so guarded them all day and through the night.

Dad

The knight in fine armor who guarded my
childhood never owned a steed but went from
city streetcar to countryside Dodge coupe
when he married my mother and began
to plant crops that continue to grow strong.

"How are you?" we ask and without fail
he answers *"Grumpy, Mean, Ornery."*

All is well. He may be bruised from a fall
but he mows the lawn, smokes his one-pipe-a-
day on the porch, gossips with friends and guards
the neighborhood while continuing to
check his crops once weekly, guardian still.

Happiness! Children, grandchildren, in-laws
and new great grandchild—all return his love.

Horses

Black Beauty
Harlequin Hullabaloo
My Friend Flicka

Dumbo

Beauty
and the Beast

Hide
and Seek

Running
and Falling

Bleeding
Toes and Heels

Boiling cauldrons
of Step Mothers

Kissing doesn't
always heal.

Our Storyteller

Night time is hers; she brings the creatures there
like animal gumdrops coming alive or
rainbows looking for a place to light and endow with gold.

She tells stories on the flying carpet
in the living room or in caves made from
blankets on tables and she crawls in, her flashlight on and off.

Does anyone know a story? She asks
and waits because sometimes we do have one
from older kids who enjoy frightening us, but she tames it.

"Shh," she says. *"Here comes the LION. Rowrrr."*
She makes us giggle and feed him a cookie
with yellow M&Ms or an orange gumdrop with sugar.

Lion is sad and needs food, friends and fun
so the adventure begins with shipmates
and tons of treasure guarded by dragons, lions in their masks.

We name colorful treasures Lion guards
laughing and outdoing each other with
full stores of party, technology, and music and forget

This is night time and it is hers to pluck
from the air and spin into golden gifts
for dragons, lions, friends, parents and us in worlds without fear.

Meeting the Night

Their bedtime was before the sun
disappeared behind its glow—
snacks and story were pre-dark
as were tuck-in and dream time.
Rarely did they visit night on purpose or befriend dark.

Now night sneaks up on them,
seeps in to wrap them in sound--
tympani and bassoons—so
they tuck blankets under toes
and pull them over their eyes as if dark could not see them.

I tell them stories, I who
have fallen in love with night
so my eyes open to join
its stars, my ears rejoice
at its music and my hands enjoy touching its heart.

And they agree to stay up
to meet and greet the dark night
with me. Soft, we kneel on rugs
beneath the picture window
on a moonless night and rest our foreheads on its coolness.

Blankets puddle around us
in case we need their safety
but instead of lifting them
we hold hands and sing *twinkle*
twinkle little star and find sparkling eyes studying us.

Ghost Story

She never slept alone
what with the goblins
in the walls and trolls
under the bed and ghosts
in the closet. In terror
she cocooned herself,
wound blankets around
so no skin and not a strand
of hair betrayed her presence.
And don't breathe. Until
one came who breathed
comfort and who loosened
the fears that bound her
and slipped in cool when
she was hot and warm when
she was cool, toes mingling
with toes, face to face.
with a coo like a mother
and words like a lover
and a touch to remove head-
aches and tension lines
so her rest was sound.
Who can compete? You
who think to embrace
her loneliness and ground
her nights would be
one too many, too long
has this charm calmed her
nights without questions
without weeping, with-
out demands or speaking.

Anchors

Here's the thing, love, she's comfortable
with ghosts. Her own especially. When
she shuts down computer and TV
and completes her Quaker rosary
she pulls the tiny anchors attached
to her soul: one hand-embossed copper
box floats her grandmother into place,
her ghost cutting hard ceramic tiles
and looking up to say *"You're only*
as old as you feel" with a toothless
grin. None of her ghosts has teeth to bite
her life, but they occupy, they stay.

Grandpa's ghost held her hand to reveal
another land of tunnel and mist
but let it go to stand young and tall
in his portrait again on the wall.
The white geese—or is it swans? bid her
retrace her days as teacher-poet
on school-year Fridays that beckon *Now*
is time to write. Still it's time—Friday
or not. Ghostly days and their careers
visit her here. I've had the hundred-
object tour, but there are more. Walk here,
hear her crowd whisper, hear her reply.

Guest Bedroom

Visiting parents brings sleep surrounds of
canvases and books, leaves and trees, music
and embroidery, piggy banks and used
Christmas and Chanukah cards—nothing is
wasted in the art of recycling, not
even old clothes turned into crazy-quilt
and hooked-rug materials.

Visiting means deep sleep in home-made dreams
prompted by newness once old but never
unwanted, delicate paintings on dried
used teabags gifted by a friend, photos
used as bookmarks, sketches and etchings from
high school art classes and trolley car rides,
brushes and paint and tape, too.

Visiting means getting tired from talking
and walking memory lanes and new paths,
hearing less and less while speaking louder
and louder during show-and-tell and look-
it-up and wait-until-you-see-what I
have been working on in the guest bedroom—
just make yourself at home.

Lake Mohonk

The dust of the path fell from her shoes each time
she raised one foot to put it in front of the other.
She lifted her head to see up the hill where a bench sat
on the precipice to a cliff. One step, two, she slowed
even more knowing her goal was in sight; she slowed
and thanked the birds cheering her on, trees sheltering
the birds, rain feeding the trees, clouds sparing the rain,
Great Father curving over all like a feather and Great Mother
willing all this should be. The bench was inhabited
by an elderly man who held a retriever on a leash.
"Sit down," he said *"and he'll fetch you a bone."*

> Time etched the spring
> whence sunshine and story flowed
> until the dark rose.

Olana

Mom and I recognize Hudson River
School of Painting's tint
far below in gold glow
feeding lush green hills
cut long ago from volcanic rock
in mountain silhouettes.

Olana on a sunny May Day
flirts with Japanese
iris and oak leaves
while tiny spiders
visit our picnic
like ants—and artists
open their easels and palettes of blue,
yellow, purple, white.

We sit on twisted grape vine benches
brown against Moroccan
tiles and nature's art.
I take notes for poems
and my companion
sketches tree stumps cut close to earth as if
its bones were showing.

I see gathering storm clouds carrying
pagan gods toward
us as if we had
entered the primal
imagination,
creators of gods, mountains, and
the small life between.

Echo

On a precipice with fall leavings
barely held together by evergreens
and the Hudson River smaller
than a ribbon far below—
Here no disguise remains; wind tears
masks off with hats, crowns, bobby-pins
and the ash of the old Mountain
House of past presidential fame.
We stand on missing pillars and
imagine we're on the sinking
Titanic—menus, music and
drowning people surround us few
on-lookers, dogs and random campers.

No birds chirp or fly, though a hawk
circles above, huge and hungry.
Who mows this scrawny grass slanted
one way? *ONE WAY* answers the echo.
Have we been faithful? Forgiving?
Kind? Grateful for open sky, blue
days and protection as we walk
the edge of the world and seasons?
We look at each other in this
landscape and answer *YES, Yes, yes.*
To everything visible and
invisible, alive and dead,
done and yet to be. *Yes.*

The Drive

Up 23A
and over
Haines Falls,
Tannersville,
Hunter and
Windham
and down—
clouds walk
curbside on
narrow
roads
crowding cars
at hairpin curves
into cliff edges,
boulders and
cascade thrills
before becoming
famous pea soup fog
in the Hudson River Valley
cradle of apple harvests
light houses and artists.

Driving up
and down,
Dad grins at danger
and I join ghost trees
floating out
beyond headlights' reach to re-imagine
headless horsemen and Rip Van Winkle.
Seated in the front
we share stories
and sensations from
separate glories.

On Fire

The sun
lit up my heart
and stayed for
the slow train ride south
in noon's short shadow,
woods to the left and
river to the right.

My heart-tree
is burning red.
There has never been
a greener day
to see it through
poet eyes and
gospel tones.

Happy heart
to branch out
beyond its four chambers
and stretch into
flame-centered sky
so bright that
air vibrates.

I expect it to burst
into song lyrics.
Instead, it crackles
earth's protective
cloud cover
to dazzle
the full moon.

In the Poppies

California pop-
pies remember me playing
once upon a time.

They told mother
they would hold and keep me young
and they kept their word.

Today, I went to
the field and listened to them
rustle around me.

Inner Child

I should have loved you more back then
when forehead furrows wanted seeds,
squinting eyes needed hugs to see,
wrinkled nose craved sweetness and cake.

None of our books showed how to love
self quietly without the crowds
praising grades and performances—
You couldn't do it by yourself.

But now, let me reach in to say
you were awesome! And you still are—
I hear the earth turning from you
and I write down secrets you hold.

You didn't know then that you knew
secrets, that you depended on
gravel, trees and reindeer moss for
stories and sensuality.

But you were in training fields for
our spirit to awaken—and
dirt, dolls, climbing trees and dress up
expanded our *Golden Book* tales.

Interlude One ~ Breaking

Tear Connection

Fibrous tissue entered my healthspeak when
knee sprains, breast cysts and a belly tumor
set off my world rocker.

I dare not shrug with fibromyalgia—
neural, not fibrous—conducting the dance
of limp, sleep and swallow.

I wish I'd studied Latin, wish I'd known that
medicine like the early Catholic
Church scorned vernacular.

But I hold my medications close and
my pain prayer closer, knowing proof will
be in the body moves.

When I medicate I might miss clues to
cause and cure but I move.   When I
pray I am still as palms.

Hospital Easter

Laparoscopy Thursday
is the first miracle:
a no-cut tumor removal
and then
stomach drain through nose
Friday.

Saturday flowers
are the second miracle:
spring with tulips and more—
more than enough to make a hat
(what I pee into
to measure my fluids).

Long snaky tube slithering
out Easter along with the promise
of Sunday resurrection
after stomach resection.

Coffee is the third miracle:
Sips, mere sips
bring hope for more life.

This Too Shall Pass

Spring blooms in crystal miniature vase, soccer ball and
grinning get-well-soon bear sit near the mirror,
black coffee and hospital socks on the trans-pal IV hanger,
two soft-drink cups with limp melted ice water and this laptop
comprise the world on this side of the divide.

Mary has the window seat where there may be sun—
a 99-year-old reminder of grandmother, also a Mary—
a do-it-herself-Mary who, blessedly, also doesn't blare TV.
She yells *"OW OW OW"* when her leg joint pings, pain a big
surprise:

"I never imagined such pain" she muses
"and it makes it hard to start in the morning"
Is it hard to walk? *"It's hard to get started."*

"Walked out this morning and cold slapped me in the face,"
adds in the cleaning lady and just then the loudspeaker female
calmly asks for emergency response in the second floor elevator
while routines continue: blood taking and medicine
and breakfasts delivered—mine broth and water ice.

Liquids slap me in the face again and again, but
Mary had a big pancake breakfast and announces it again.

When I walk out tomorrow morning, I will feel real air
caress through scents' onslaught, after a week of bubbling
air flow and liquid IVs, my submission a prayer to healing:
"Let the Doctor's hand be steady, let my body accept the cure."

Doctors took part of my stomach and now I wait
for hard waste to pass through
as Mary relieves herself three times overnight and again today.

"Mary, Mary, quite contrary, how does your garden grow?"
"Well, well, can't you tell? I live long and love it so!"

When I am 99 and pain makes it hard to start, I want to be like Mary,
my garden of spring blooms lined up so failure is surprise
and my voice is strong enough to brag or call out *"OW OW OW."*
(When I am old and wise enough and this too has passed
into the low valley of memory with its flowers and weeds.)

Walking That Dog

GIST
Feels like spit at the t-tip
of the tongue: G.I.S.T.
unless rolled out in fullness:
gastro
intestinal
stromal
tumor.

Feels like nothing
a small lesion of soft tissue
just a hiccup in
connective tissue
but a sarcoma
nonetheless
rare
but there.

Feel it now
the word I didn't know
applied: cancer
did not breathe through me
I did not think it or walk it
as if a dog I had but didn't like
because it drooled
and panted and
demanded.

Feel alarm and relief
instantly: it was and it is
no longer. The lab report
says . . . Hold. Exhale.
Hear my forward-thinking
oncologist surgeon

had cut larger than tumor size
leaving clean edges—
It's all gone.

Try to feel gist-less and re-started
after cancer's visit,
startled from the cloud of unknowing
long enough to cut my air on
what might have been.
Yes, we'll check and recheck.
And I will know
GIST-less—
maybe walk her
and pet her.

Recovery

No reason exists for this life I am
on carnal plains of earth with its playthings
its means of both healing and destruction.

This elastic band of a life stretched taut
with threat to internal organs and then
released but not to its glib former shape.

Escape got my attention, gave me pause
to measure listless randomness against
some grace and to find chance lacking in rhyme.

But reason provides meter only, no
sense nor nonsense matches the spirit of
being—seen now or not. I am spirit.

And that this truth belies all gloom and doom
does not negate how rarely joy finds room.

Prelude

Still on wobbly legs from convalescence,
I plan to see azalea bud and maples
burst on the cemetery path with mixed
grass and evergreen between sepulcher
and chiseled stone.

   I will join robins there
and unidentified fly-bys tweeting
with all their hearts—always live music on
the cemetery path where no dogs plop
and few cats roam.

   I and my friend will
hobble by newly placed wreaths and people
alone, cars unlocked and near for quick get-
aways under the always blue and bright
canopy of sky designed to contrast
realms below with sunbeams rising behind
clouds lit by mystery.

   I have seen ghostly escalators
up and down, but not the riders I know
must be near rainbow which—rain or shine—is
there against blue on the cemetery path I'll
walk today to watch unseen artists play.

On the Train

Ability to travel again!
Unexpected
joy paramount where
depression reigned.
Window seat and beyond
snowscape in bright sun
frozen chunks lining deep
purple water channel.
Sentinel trees
watch sun skip like stones
on wavy lapping water.
Everything is new
shouting "*Look at Me!*"
Look at me!
Look at me looking—
Me! Escaped prisoner
of my body
taking it with me
over the river and
through the woods
to my family's home
on this train.

On the Cusp

Today came the moment/day/week I love
just before spring's buds and leaf curls are large
enough to see, when trees glow/shimmer/smile
in hazy color—all pink/green/gold/brown—
portent of lushness to come; and I am
entranced through the changes of daylight and
must pull myself away wondering if
I/we/people appear thus, on the cusp
of enlightenment/revelation/love?

On the Journey to Enlightenment

She met a man who created beauty
in sand drawings he let wind blow away.

She met a mixed-breed pup whose loyalty
and love knew no bounds in life or in death.

She met a rock that stubbed her toe without
moving from her path, without eroding.

She met a stranger who held her hand through
pain and sadness without knowing her name.

She met a tree who called her name and let
her climb for vision and sour apples.

She met a woman who increased goodness
by finding three causes for hope each day.

She met herself in a gasp of surprise
and laughter among the lines of her songs.

Shaping and Sounding

This valley is shaped like Yo-Yo's cello
that plays sun and shade and bread and butter
without fail, counting on itself through time.

I know it is one of the mother's backs
one of the Bible's depths, one layer of
regeneration—citied or countried.

When I open my mouth, its sounds pour out—
or so I wish—inviting all peoples
to travel here in spirit and partake.

This valley is my intention, calling
me in, calling you too, to voice our love
in music's international soundings.

Imagine

Come into my arms and let me love you.
Earth, sky and I exchange greetings daily.
Cognizant of what we are not saying:
We are one. And how could it be other?

Wise, we still pretend to oblivion—
flaw of our divine tragi-comedy—
to ignore our kinship in the kingdom
we say we want but do not find ever.

You are my arms, forehead, ever-seeing
gaze. No other God or Heaven exists,
yet we make this Hell with a frustrating
willfulness, eager to avoid the signs.

Why?

Think how joyous for you and me just
to open our arms and let life love us.

Interlude Two ~ Healing

People of Continually Flowing Waters

Every river speaks of lost nations—
their dinner menus, dwellings and crossings:

Here on the Schuylkill, it's the Lenape
forgotten, and on the Hudson River
where I was born, it's Mohican.

My folks hail from Eurasian rivers—Rhine,
Mosel and Volga—which we've forgotten.

And if we remembered?

And added people of the Euphrates, Congo,
Nile, Amazon and Rio Grande?

Added color from every river!

Let people of every river bring potluck
to our tables and add their purest
drinking water to a common fountain.

Let the celebration commence!

We are free of pollution and full of
respect. We are eager to listen to
each other's stories and enrich our own.
We dedicate ourselves to rivers' flow.

Tree Branches

Lie flat on your bare back; look up through me
as I tat curtains that shield Sun from you
and you from Sun. The two of you compete
foolishly when my love for both is true.

Nature wrote root and crown of me to share
as heart of all that's here. I need sunlight
to live and water, soil and air to spare—
and I need you to tend me and delight

in reading me morn, noon and night. You read
me through four seasons round so your strong heart
with mine resounds and creates art we need
to praise the grand design of which we're part.

Together we wake those too blind to see—
earth lives longer when you distinguish me.

Tree's Gift

Look into my nooks
to see the heart and sapwood
of childhood, rings where sun
and water fed me.
You inherit this pith.

Whisper wishes into my
leaf buds and blossoms;
lay your cheek against my bark.
I will teach you to
laugh and join nature's gala.

When I exist in
museums only, will you sing
with winds and dance with rain?
Will you still find cloud
steps rooted in good earth?

Unframed

To speak of mountain beauty
frame our outlook with
sedimentary boulders,
shrubs and rusty leaves
of oak and sumac
looking down on
evergreen and dark
shadows of white
strato-cumulus clouds
freeze framed
in blue sky above.

This is to say nothing
of the unframed
solidity beneath feet,
popping wind in ears
and swallow, slight ache
in eyes grasping images
that leap lightly from
heart to spirit.

A different angle
would include
humans too.

Humans

Unlike trees, all mammals have white skeletons.
Unlike trees, all mammals have deep dark red blood,
and foot bone connected to the ankle bone,
ankle bone connected to the leg bone,
leg bone connected to the knee bone.

Like little ceramic doll limbs joined
by sinews to move, bones are not flexible
themselves. Mammals imitate saplings
bending in the wind, pushed or pulled
by curiosity, but flexing requires synapses

connecting to response centers, muscles,
and nerves. Unlike trees, humans need
practice leaning in and touching
so they can stand tall in time.

Happiness

A beautiful, strong tree says
I am unique!

Unique the form and veins of my skin, unique.

*The leaves in my branches and the smallest scar on my bark
reveal the Eternal in me.*

My labor is holy.

*Life is not easy, not difficult.
Those are childish thoughts.*

*You are anxious because your path leads away from home.
Home is within you, or home is nowhere at all.*

*Every path leads homeward,
every step is birth, death, mother.*

The tree rustles thoughts, long-breathing and restful,
wiser than we. Listen.

*No longer want to be a tree.
want to be nothing except what you are.*

*That is home.
Happiness.*

Carpe Diem

God spits out
cherry blossom poetry
along with Mother Nature
as if they're shaking
the edges of a vast
urban counterpane
to entertain us all.

You'd think their voices
would be louder, but
they let color take center stage,
petals make the deepest bows
and the winds create
bouquets to honor
spring's performance.

How quickly the pink
blossoms come and go—
their curtain falls.
Yet divine courtship
bears fruit of deeper hue,
flesh wrapped pits so sweet
we chew and spit a few.

Sand in the Shell

The stainless steel fork on my porch
gets flatter and fatter each week.

They forgot to soak the entire
cabbage to drive out living worms.

I don't remember why it is
so urgent to capture this poem.

I said to myself: *Now. Now! Do.
It. Now.* I have fork and cabbage.

Oh! Crisp autumnal air lifts me—
Oh! I crave coffee and apples.

Cinnamon. Pie crust and pumpkins.
Mulled cider. Wooden spoons. Sweet aches.

Diabetic, I count sugars
and cholesterol but not smell.

They can't take that away—scents and
memories fading out like ghosts—

Irritations fading in like
concrete forks and cabbage worms.

Light and Shadow

You romp around shoulders and eyelashes
partners of my afternoon nap.

You cloak me with *chiaroscuro* through drapes
parted like deep-valleyed mountains.

You tattoo my smooth skin and sign your work
with finger edges of decades.

My wrinkles relax in your scrutiny,
my heart is fearless at your touch.

Part Two ~ Aging

The Dream

Product of the radical seventies and one decade late, I

donned my turtle hood to exit luxury, traveling light
and slow back to the proverbial road not taken.

"Halt the erosion of truth," Grandmother called
from her White House upon the hill, where she sat
typing out letters and letting them fall.

Evergreen trees lined the night as Australia
became a no-nuke zone and an actor aligned
his springtime in America to re-organize the right
and Grandmother wrote *"Dear Editor"* from her remote site.

I, Turtle, moved slowly through acres of passivity
while fateful animals piled earth on my shell
and played out the original rite of creativity.

Grandmother called out for my group to smite
the Pharaoh and his henchmen—like Moses to fight.

The living image stays now though I close my eyes to sleep:
old women awake in a tower, turtle inching straight,
pharaoh underground spinning orders that make
wrinkled hands type letters, clocks tick, bosses take,
money move, truth die, turtles walk, I sleep at night.

My eyes focused upward, I see her steady Light.

We'll Meet Again

Wild, swinging through trees God gave me, I did
not seek out love, intelligence, fun, joy
or gain but tried to touch ground to calm once
between passions' open-door obstacles.

I twinkled at living dangerously
on edgy movements for freedom of speech,
race equality, equal access to
education, affirmative action ...

Stop killing each other in undeclared
war, *start* Head Start, *end* alley abortion,
make birth control available, *free* love,
free food, *free* truth, *let* rock musicians live,
hold me, help me, I'll help, I'm here always.

Community women, we roared inside
and sang aloud, separately strengthened,
we returned for peace, justice and nuclear-
free zones; but I froze, closed and locked my door.

A teacher, I listened and fed the roar
inside alone sometimes—but sight lines dimmed
and aging zoned while I watched for signs that
youth might organize and we'd meet again.

Dark, Declined

Addiction is a dark hole;
not finding God where we look
daily is darker; and loss
of faith is darkest of all.
I say fill in the hole as
if a minor street repair,
but spirited counselors
provide opposite advice.
My stop-smoking teacher spoke
of a learning curve: *See hole
and fall in. Climb out, leave and
turn back to fall in again.*

> *Choose to avoid the dark hole—
> walk around its siren calls
> closer and closer until
> falling in the hole again.*

> *Plan another route to walk
> neither near nor in view of
> the dark, darker and darkest
> holes that plague like birds of prey.*

I leave the dark holes, turn to
stranger pathways and knock on
unknown doors—where surprise leads
beyond old patched-up crises.
I know I will return some
day as tourist or tour guide,
and even bring a ladder
to descend into the dark—
and ascend willingly once
more in gratitude for maps
I find there, for queries that
showed me the way to the light.

Finding Balance

I do not balance, I am
broken open from falling—
and that—as the song says—is
how the light gets in with its
daily dose of strength, hope and
desire. I want to sit in
front of trucks and run wild through
wars to block operators
from destroying my neighbors.

I cannot run now, and could
not sit when young. Instead, I
broke open like buds in my
garden and spilled light into
classrooms where I learned to sing
along and sing alone with
my own and borrowed words—to
counter balance in contact
improv blooming and spilling

hope into community
banks and gardens, voice born
from protective silence and
joined to empowerment in
a potent solution we all
can use. Broken and out of
balance, I contact balance
with words I could never find,
write or move into alone.

October

October was my favorite month:
fall leaves and harvest,
Ramadan and New Year
and finally, as nights get longer,
Halloween.
As a little girl I dressed up:
cowboy, princess, cloud and rainbow
and shyly opened my bag for elderly hands
with candy and cooing
So Sweet!

And then when kids my age walked
in hoods with chalk, socks,
eggs and water balloons
I put away the candy and gauze.
Halloween
became Mischief Night
and like a tarnished gold coin
I slipped away to hide and pray
Don't let the cat out!
Lock the garage.
Remember that year the heat ducts were filled
with shaving cream and egg?
Don't answer the door!
Because *"knock knock"*
"Who's there?"
Mischief Night.
What more?
Hell itself.
Maybe Death.

Dad used to tell a story
about Death and a miraculous old man
who ate a bulb of garlic every night before bed

so when Death came to call
and tapped him on the shoulder
He turned around to yell *Whoooo's theeeeere?*
and fumed Him away
with his breath.

I eat the garlic, but
I do not fear Death in his normal guise.
I fear undisguised Youth
and an absence of Soul.
Hell is the growing Child with no moral sense
Hell is the Mischief Child who figures out
we don't bounce back like in cartoons
and likes it—
who parties to the sound of pain and
cannot be fumed away.

October was my favorite month
with brilliant leaves flying and
harvests feeding multiple Thanksgivings
and Jewish New Years and Ramadan—
Holy and Peaceful
in the lengthening dark—

> *Dearest child*
> *give me back*
> *my October nights.*

Lavender

Talking about my lavender—
Gardener's Hand Repair Cream,
essential oil for tension headaches,
underwear drawer liners and
messy woody bushes in the front yard,
(the ones that call the bees) —
Don't knock it if you ain't tried it.
Telling me it's an old women's smell
telling me it tickles your nose—well
g'wan then and let it tickle
g'wan and sneeze. *God Bless You.*

Let me tell you about my lavender
that the bees love so much—watch them
happily drink and drunken, wobble home.
They won't sting you so full, but if they do,
this very flower will heal the wound
and calm your nerves. The buds
is what does it, the pretty purple buds
that I use to extract the essential oils,
that I use to stuff the pillows against
tired eyes and anxious dreams and
restlessness that takes you wandering
far from me, young'un, *far from me.*

If it makes you think of an old woman,
let it remind you of me and the hours
we spent gathering sweet clover and
lavender honey, clarifying and spooning
it onto the bread we baked—a feast
for all the senses. If it makes you think
of old women, think of the joys of a long life
to witness the changes of a century or so.
This can be yours while lucid and mobile

if you remember to bring along fresh garlic
and the honey the bees give you,
bees covered, like me, in lavender.

Small Change

Pennies, nickels and dimes
don't fit parking meters,
no longer pay for thoughts
and do not chime on the
golden ring of union
as fingers reach deeply
into last year's pockets
for sustenance and love.

I find these coins rolling
on classroom hardwood floors,
scoop them into my wish
jar and watch them grow just
as I watch bits of now
and then accumulate
in youthful minds and bloom
perennial gardens.

My Mother's Day

My neighbor passed me on the way to church,
lace on her thick white hair and red on her lips.
"Last Saturday I turned 90," she grinned at me
as I hugged her. *"I live next to a church—*
But my own church is way across town."
Off she wove on her delight-filled mission,
having turned down her son's offer of a lift.

My own mother is way across the mountains preparing
grapefruit and raisin bread for breakfast with Dad
who checks his sugar with one pinprick and plans
their drive downriver to Kingston where they buy fruit
and water before turning North to the gallery opening
in Woodstock: Two of her paintings hang there.

Childless, I grow old amid the elderly who stand like trees
and let me sit under their spreading green limbs
while their seedlings sprout through the debris
of years that has fallen away. Like reptiles, they split
and slide out of old skin, revealing new beauty.

A Spinster's Tale

"Nicely spun" my readers say and instantly I become Charlotte
using my web for the welfare of others while waiting
for the two facts of life: offspring and death.

I am told that they come at the same moment
and have to remind myself that though I am a spinster
I am not a spider. Spider is just my avatar.

And my house is home to multiple spiders
whose webs hold it together, and whose yarns
I overhear from the edge of sleep:

*Do we truly have a safe harbor? A human being
who asks first and shoos later? Who
has a brush for a hand instead of a rock? Who
cares more about the yarn than the trap?
and can we stay and un-spin our luggage
shouting as if from Whosville: listen, listen, if only,
hear us and meet us and do not eat us
and we will spin your tales into gold and
decorate your bookshelves? World without end.*

My tenants have already traced their paths from
children's books into poetry and the classics.

One recent waking dawn they asked me to write a play
in which Charlotte, Anansi and Ariadne meet
for a beauty contest with a human judge.

I said *I am not interested in world politics,*
but they said *This is our home, and we are
your blessings, speak.*

And my tuffet became their daily
hang out and drop in while I spun
with ink as my yarn or the word processor on.

Nightly, too, I spin and spin, then let
words steep ... and the spiders
move my fingers while I sleep.

Self Portrait with Spider

I killed a spider in the shower, on the bathtub rim.
I tried not to—

Pushed at it first with my finger, praying it to be easy
but I hadn't seen the short puddle blocking safety
and after, she lay on her back curling her legs in.

I shifted her to dry terry; she pulled her legs tighter.
I thought there was a chance, but no, and this was not the long
life and companionship I had promised.

I squeeze back tears.

I face truth in the mirror, eyes resting on my little nose, tracing
eyebrows and high Russian cheek bones, shallow cheeks,
wrinkled lip lines and neck under sharp chin.

I have time, I think, time to become benign and then I'll be able
to lift my chin and look into my eyes again.

Ode to Books

Even as I plot
to deplete you
I love you
You who are
weight
and substance
of every stage
in my journey.

You are stages
awakened
in my hands
revealing
to my senses
the sweetest
efforts of multiple
workers: each
part of you
lovingly made
from the inventions
of centuries of seekers
to hallow
the few names
gracing your
front covers.

Covers
oft covered
with thin sheets
of artistic
illustration
crisp and inviting
over spines
straight as arrows

that are useful
even and especially
when broken.

Broken open at hinges
you are each a portal
to an author's universe
that builds on, expands
and surrounds your
elders, refusing
to abandon them
preferring tribal respect
over execution—
every tribe has errors
and learning curves.

The curve of your
pages when riffled!
Can anything be sexier?
Smooth smooth
the touch of each
leaf turning
under my fingers
some crisp and ashen
from age or cheapness
but all covered
with symbols
that tap away at
brain cells and hearts
of we who dare
your borders.

I have dared more,
dear ones: your

borders and margins
are my memory
timeline
of responses:
you can read me there
when I was parrot
to the author,
when I began questioning,
when I entered into dialogue
with the history of ideas.

You, dear books
are my history
and if I remove
some chapters
it is only to make
room for more
and to accept
new technologies
of production,
more nameless inventors
building beautiful
new scaffolding for
your job, now
that the materials
that built you
are disappearing
from our earth.

Alone At Last

Inside her room the unmade bed beckons
smelling of bleach and quilted blue feathers.
A leafy breeze calls her to the open
window, the dormer seat invites her time.

When she closes her door, the zephyr rests
on her writing desk, flips through paper piles
of words spilled from her printer to the floor
mouths open, hungry and calling for food.

Be patient, she breathes as she sits to see
songbirds talking outside in the maples
then leans back, eyes closed, to nestle into
God's embrace, rest her skeleton, quiet.

Entering worship is easier than
falling asleep lately, she notes, smiling
at the welcome, imagining her heart
opening to its light and its darkness.

Faces of family members and friends
blink by her sub consciousness, and she holds
them each—struggles and all—in light and strength
and gratitude, feeling for ministry.

And then, she reaches for notebook and pen,
she approaches her desktop computer
and writes about the parallels among
intentional sleep, worship and writing.

It is as if, she writes, *I ask for voice—*
one of my own—and find it has been here
waiting for me to awake wholly and
grasp it, to risk sound and be visible.

We are all, she writes, *the same animal*
flesh divided and shaped to different
purposes. If you do it, I do it,
no need for jealousy. We all do it.

God needs us, she writes, *to see creation*
as reciprocal. We form each other—
rulers and ruled, masters and slaves, privileged
and un-, female and male—and we can re-form.

There is no "they," she ponders in dream-like
nudes descending staircases splitting on
each step into dozens more until they
crowd her into floating away with them.

They descend from window to ground, from sky
to city and rise in accents darker
and lighter, blacker and whiter, seeking
roofs to sleep under, seeking safe places.

Back in her room, she detaches changed from
worship and writing, ready for sleeping,
ready to dream, she hopes, how to achieve
the equality that her truth reveals.

Peace

My door is locked
a friend is home downstairs
kitty's ears flicker in her dreams
and words settle firmly here
while the blue chair swivels
tea kettle begins to boil
and a clean cup waits
with loose chamomile
in its strainer.

Piles of paper chores
and books surround me,
but it is late to call the President
or Congress--and Democracy
can wait another day while
people put away phones
and food, and I stack
my dirty dishes
until morning.

Midnight cars pass slowly,
lamp in the window glows
small in the darkness,
sleep softens the gravity
pull of hundreds of neighbors
whose consciousness buzzes
into my thoughts.

Now I am alone
like in prayer.

Neighbors

*It is the time you have wasted for your rose
that makes your rose so important.*
~ Antoine de Saint-Exupéry

If everyone had a little planet
with a flower, we could truly begin.
Think of it: *Everyone 'neath his vine and
fig tree shall live in peace and unafraid.*
Little planets make good neighbors, places
to go to be alone or with loved ones,
inviolate homes that need us to "waste
time" there between curiosity in-
duced explorings, magnets to pull our eyes
out to the stars, each special to someone.
If everyone had a little planet
with a flower, we could truly begin
to tame the blossoms and let them take us
to love and life in peace and unafraid.

Oh! I Must Be Dreaming

oh! I must be dreaming
thinking of poetry club in its honest laughter
being told that I could not rap
that I couldn't keep the beat and
how painful when topics
just don't belong in the song.
I smile just thinking of the days
we laughed at the otherness
in the safety of a room
in an unsafe school
in a crazy world
where children pay the price over and over
for no reason at all but
                    oh! I must be dreaming
because I have a vision
that religions fade and the Holy wipes memories—
people in a daze shake hands and hug neighbors to their hearts
and take down walls before any other work at all comes to mind
and never mind because this day is a spiritual celebration of the
revelation that all men are brothers and sisters too with nothing
to prove
and everything to gain by playing.
                    oh! I must be dreaming
this new game, insane, really shooting up the brain
with love and restitution, no retribution
and no Americanization despite
the rising sensation of enough food and shelter for all,
no helter skelter, no more early death because we tossed
the economic underpinnings of disaster that hid behind religion
when poverty was the real killer and truth could kill poverty
any time the walls fell and the bell rang the knell on the CEOs
bringing in the bacon cut from the hides of children and now

oh! I must be dreaming
at national boundaries people hang out welcome signs
and dismantle military lines, bullets, shrapnel and land mines
before inviting Mother Nature to produce chem-free food
that first does no harm and second makes us full of stories
to give each other before sleeping safely at last,
the only blast, a late party with music and dance celebrating
peace at last and while we sleep the green grows tall,
trees take over roads and slow down all
whispering new charms at last: *no speed, no rush, no scarcity.*
                    Let's move right on.

Waking

I must have pulled the blanket up during the night
the one weighted on me past dawn, hugging, holding
clinging (oh-let-me-stay) my shawl to the window
where it continues over road and hedge and cars
as the heavy white laid down while I slept deeply.

I love these moments of unbroken mood, textured
in every substance, drenching all in mystery.
I float in it down the stairs to slow motion morning
routines and see even the minute and second
hands of time dancing to its warm and loving grace.

Knowing this blanket will melt into the daytime
I drink deeply, beaming *thank you* into pale day.

A Good Morning

I check blog and email
with my morning coffee
as sixty years ago
I shoved hands under
my pillow to check if
Tooth Fairy visited
and slid down banisters
to see what Santa left
under the Christmas tree
and where Easter Bunny
hid the eggs and candy.

Smiling at the magic
lies of childhood and youth,
reflecting on maturity,
I read and respond
before opening
curtains and blinds.

Ancient Kitty

My ancient kitty sits tall and still as a sphinx
gazing at me with her clear celadon eyes—
measuring me, memorizing me, saying to
me *"Hey there. I love you"* with a spiritual
softness that is new.
                              She has turned a corner
in her life—sleeping more than she's awake, alert
to meal and playtimes out of habit rather than
need, looking for dark quiet places to curl up
and dream of pleasures.
                              I show her my gratitude
for the latest of her gifts—feline fortitude—
by gazing back, combing her itchy places and
giving her more time and touch without lifting her—
Oh my darling cat! You don't complain at each new
disability—
                              You simply go on and on
as is your job and mine: live life to the fullest!
I did not anticipate learning this from you,
my dear. Have I given you enough love and food?
Have you felt my affection through your fur and my
skin, touching, being?

My Garden Grows

I am a garden with room for the life
and death of annuals, perennials,
sturdy shrubs and fragile stems, fullness and
fallow-ness, blooms and buds.

I am a garden, no doubt, nurtured by
my blood family, poets, friends, teachers
and other guardians, God's messengers
of love, truth and kindness.

My garden grows because I tend to it,
too—I am spry enough for that! And
I am farmer enough to share the wealth
and bouquets of harvest.

But first, I try hard to remove harmful
isms that persist despite reason and
experience. How wonderful the thorns
that remind me.

I walk among gardens of the human
race knowing that I am surrounded by
love and beauty, though some is hidden by
negligence and weeds.

Waves

Emptying work time from my hour glass
should have left more room for visiting you, true,
but the oddest thing happened—
The more I poured out, the fuller it got. I kid you not.

The dam just burst is all:
Poems welled up every day
and people wanted to drink!
I heard strange voices, sounds, thoughts
and discovered they were mine!
Books, stacked dangerously
on pine-shelf edges, tumbled into my hands,
which felt good enough
but then they seduced me
with their smooth pages and weight and laughter.
Online, I emptied
the lesson planning and, lo!
it had been hiding radical news, satire,
poems—so many kinds—and the philosophy of creativity,
digital books and magazines and lines
and tigers and bears. O My.

I will sail to your dock after I find mine.
I am wading through the flood,
trying to sort my new wealth
into neat time segments.

You remember how I couldn't swim?
I'm getting ready to jump the next wave,
and I couldn't be happier.

Present Humor

From there to here, and here to there,
funny things are everywhere.
~ Dr. Seuss

I love how air puffs out on the first syll-
able: *h*ue, *h*umor, *h*uman, *h*uman-ness.

I love her slight smile while meditating
so delightful to balance, to ease pain.

I love the huge laugh of the newcomer
who hung out with us at last night's party.

I love the voiced aitch in *who what where why*
which join *how* to spell curiosity.

I love knock-knock jokes because I must part-
icipate, asking *Who's there?* And then *Who?*

I love finding an owl sitting above
because I heard it and then looked for it.

I love the slight differences of *hoot*
who and *hue*, feel which puffs more on your hand.

I love your company, how we can be
silly and lighten up each other's heart.

Mother's Day

Together this year, Mom and I don't wait.
Scrabble board between us, we fight our duels
with wooden tiles and stories to relate--
diving in as if starving for face time
with tea, cookies, dictionaries and words.

Wins and losses? We lost track years ago
and play as if riding teeter-totters
seriously, talking over our turns--
a dance of brightness, tea leaves and fate.

.

Bio

Poet Susan Chast is originally from upstate New York. She attended Coxsackie-Athens Central School in the Mid-Hudson Valley before moving to Worcester, MA, to finish high school and earn her BA at Clark University. Concerns for equality and the quality of freedom drew her into the feminist and peace movements of the 1970s and 80s and this activist experience fueled her philosophy of education.

Dedicated to participatory education, she earned a Master of Arts in Liberal Studies from Wesleyan University in Middletown, CT, a Masters in Theater from SUNY Albany and finally, a PhD in Dramatic Art from the University of California at Berkeley. She has taught theater and language arts in community, high school and college venues.

Retired now, Susan Chast is luxuriating in time to write. She blogs at *Susan's Poetry* and is an active member of the online community *Poets United.* Her poetry appears in *Tuck Magazine, Types and Shadows: Journal of the Fellowship of Quakers in the Arts, Apiary On-line, The First Day* and the 2013 edition of *The dVerse Anthology: Voices of Contemporary World Poetry.* She recently published *Taking a Walk with God: Poems by Susan Chast and Art by Jennifer Elam.*

Printed in Great Britain
by Amazon

21830689R00054